PECULIAR

A Poetry Odyssey

Edited By Roseanna Caswell

First published in Great Britain in 2021 by:

Young Writers
Remus House
Coltsfoot Drive
Peterborough
PE2 9BF
Telephone: 01733 890066
Website: www.youngwriters.co.uk

Printed and bound in the UK by BookPrintingUK
Website: www.bookprintinguk.com
YB0460C

★ FOREWORD ★

Welcome Reader!

Are you ready to discover weird and wonderful creatures that you'd never even dreamed of?

For Young Writers' latest competition we asked primary school pupils to create a Peculiar Pet of their own invention, and then write a poem about it! They rose to the challenge magnificently and the result is this fantastic collection full of creepy critters and amazing animals!

Here at Young Writers our aim is to encourage creativity in children and to inspire a love of the written word, so it's great to get such an amazing response, with some absolutely fantastic poems. Not only have these young authors created imaginative and inventive animals, they've also crafted wonderful poems to showcase their creations and their writing ability. These poems are brimming with inspiration. The slimiest slitherers, the creepiest crawlers and furriest friends are all brought to life in these pages – you can decide for yourself which ones you'd like as a pet!

I'd like to congratulate all the young authors in this anthology, I hope this inspires them to continue with their creative writing.

★ CONTENTS ★

Annabelle Coak (8)	45
Ellie Mawer (8)	46
James Anniss (8)	47
Carter Morgan (9)	48
Malachy Jordan (8)	49
Indigo Bevan (8)	50
Afsa Chowdhury (8)	51
Sofia Scrowther (8)	52
Tomasz Bis (8)	53
Abigail Rumba (7)	54
Harry Edwards (8)	55
Sienna Brace (8)	56
Thea Brace (7)	57
Katy Hill (8)	58
Joseph Thomas-Bizjak (9)	59
Mali James (7)	60
Tom Beckinsale (8)	61
Arlo Llewellyn (7)	62
Scarlett Baldwin (7)	63
Marwa Fadel (7)	64
Maisy Searle (8)	65
Ariandas Poznekovas (8)	66
Daniel Kocur (8)	67
George Evans (9)	68
Josie John (7)	69
Joshua Taylor (8)	70
Blake Johnson (8)	71
Chloe Acaster (9)	72
Libby McCabe (7)	73
Vesta Filipovas (8)	74
Ava Folley (8)	75
Ethan Ellis (8)	76
George Wyatt (7)	77
Emily Dinham (8)	78
Sam Alford (8)	79
Olivia Davidson (7)	80
Theo Morris (7)	81
Anthony Cammish (7)	82
Ollie Newman (7)	83
Amber Jarvie (7)	84
Hannah Hughes (8)	85
Kaelan Hurley (9)	86
Harri Bartlett (7)	87

George Gale (8)	88
Chase Hurley (7)	89
Charlie Harrison (7)	90
Jesse Jones (8)	91
Charlie Sims (7)	92
Jorja Payne (8)	93

St Bartholomew's CE Primary School, Stourport-On-Severn

Jasmine Breakwell (9)	94
Emily Rix (9)	95
Shannon Shurmer (8)	96
Olivia Houghland (8)	97
Kayla Cable (9)	98
Peter-Roy Winters (8)	99
Zach Williams (8)	100
Jorge Cook (8)	101
Cassie Mai Tovey (8)	102
William Stanley (8)	103
Oliver Bird (8)	104
Polly Walton (8)	105
Charlie Lippitt (8)	106
Lillie-Mae Mae Adams (8)	107
Molly Foster (8)	108
Jacob Price (8)	109
Suleekha Ibrahim (8)	110
Conor Leach (9)	111
Tobias Griffiths (8)	112
Jake Curzey (8)	113
Carlton Harper (8)	114
Alfie Short (8)	115
Ellie May Mason (8)	116
Darcie Lees (8)	117
Charlie Coglan (8)	118
Kia Sutcliffe (8)	119
Alfie Walker	120

St Edward's Catholic Academy, Swadlincote

Noah Callow (8)	121
Victoria Malinowska (8)	122
Sebastian Brown (8)	123
Ivy-Bo Fogg (8)	124

St Edward's Royal Free Ecumenical Middle School, Windsor

Raphaelle Leigh-Davies (9)	125
Clara Zuk (9)	126
Averil Newton (10)	128
Liliana Baxendale (9)	129
Elena Littlewood (10)	130
Grace Fowler (10)	131
Robyn Calver (10)	132
Olivia Rutland (10)	133

The Glapton Academy, Nottingham

Sienna Simpson (9)	134

Tiferes Shlomo Boys' School, Hendon

Yisroel Dov Bor Weitz (9)	135
Mendy Friedman (9)	136
Chaim Roth (9)	137
Shmuli Grosshass (9)	138
Chesky Feiner (9)	139
Menachem Weisz (9)	140
Sruli Tesler (9)	141
Shmuli Roth (10)	142
Chaim Heller (9)	143

Westminster Cathedral Choir School, Westminster

Alexander Vanbrabant (9)	144
Jasper Channell (9)	145
James Simpson (9)	146
Vincent Vogel (10)	147
Kei Endo (9)	148
Guanting Luo (9)	149
Laurence Stiles (10)	150
Henry Talalla (9)	151
Max Billet (9)	152
John Stoner (9)	153
Tomas Trenor (9)	154
Adam Harris (9)	155
Loïc Lenoble (9)	156
Alejandro Maqueda Martin (9)	157

THE POEMS

COME ON
SLOW
COACH

Peek-A-Dragon

I have a dragon called Yoshie-Boshie
He likes to be very bossy
When his buddies come over they're very noisy
He loves playing hide-and-seek only when they do
not peek
He likes to hide in the bushes while eating sushi
He has a little sister called Molly and her favourite
toy is her dolly
He likes to have a bit of a jolly and jump out of the
bushes to scare Molly
He always comes home when it is time for tea
And also, when he needs to pee
At the end of the day, we've had so much fun
I'll tuck him cosy in bed into a little bun.

Olivia Reid (8)

Annanhill Primary School, Kilmarnock

My Pet Trockadille

I have a pet trockadille
It loves to eat berries
There is only one in the wild
It is super rare
I love it so much
It is super kind
It has a hat on
And loves Christmas
It runs around in the snow
And makes silly noises
It will make you happy
It also likes popcorn
It is white and grey
And wears a stripy jumper
It loves getting hugs
It loves to lick you
Trockadille is really cuddly
It loves to watch movies
About Christmas
And eats popcorn

It will doze away
To sleep in your arms.

Millie Neill (8)
Annanhill Primary School, Kilmarnock

Pat The Cat

I have a pet cat named Pat
He loves to miaow and bow
He always wakes me with a *miaow, miaow, miaow*
When I open my eyes he bows in front of me
Not to let him carry my shopping because he
always starts hopping
Pat loves hats and when he goes down town he
always wears one
Pat has a mat and he loves it
He rolls and rolls on it until he makes a hole in it
Pat's favourite month of the year is December
Because the mice you can't see what he is doing
But when he comes back with some mice, lice
come following behind him.

Eilidh Muirhead (7)
Annanhill Primary School, Kilmarnock

Glitter Baby's First Competition!

My pet is a dog
It is called Glitter Baby
It is so funny
Oh, so much glitter
He is very small
He gets up at night
He lives in my bed
He swims so fast
He is so much fun
He loves me so much
He can go in a car
He is so, so small
He can dance so good
He can go to school
He can run so fast.

Jada-Jo Branney (8)
Annanhill Primary School, Kilmarnock

Drark Rules The World

D rark is a deadly beast in New York

"R oar! Roar!" said Drark

A s if it was a lion

"R oar! Roar!" again

K etchup went in his eye! Haha!

Callum Cooke (7)

Annanhill Primary School, Kilmarnock

Me And My Special Dog

Me and my funny, special dog were on a walk
Suddenly, it turned night-time
And we got lost in the park
It was very dark
I tapped my dog on the nose
And her eyes lit up like a torch
I got on her back
And she flew into the sky to my delight
I could not believe my eyes
Me and my dog flying in the sky
It was not long before we found our home
In the garden, there was a gnome
In through the window, we both went
Laying down our sleepy heads in our beds.

Sarah Cretch (8)
Beechwood Primary Academy, Southway

Ruby Tail Fury

Up goes the everlasting fury of the infamous ruby tail,
it whips over the golden hexagon plated shell.
Covered by golden delight is ocean blue dog fur
concealing pitch-black skin.

Further up is the famously long giraffe neck,
leading to a bronze cat-sized head.
Down to the torso are dark purple legs,
under these pillars of strength are feet the size of eels.

My creature is known as the Tortapuss,
a rare showcase of mother nature's power.
It is feared throughout society,
with its venomous white tongue.

So watch out for this creature
or you will be its next victim.

Jacob Moore (11)
Cedar Integrated Primary School, Crossgar

George Jar Jar Binks

My cat is the most annoying cat in the world
Because he starts to sing at midnight
He is called George and sings
Jar Jar Binks thousands of times
My cat annoys everyone in the whole world
Suddenly he stops singing at 12 o'clock
George is hungry, I am happy.

Adam Hood (10)
Evergreen Primary School, Bishop Auckland

All About My Dog

She's cute and lovely
Lazy and grumpy
She's furry and sassy
Clumsy and scared of the wall
She licks my foot
And it makes me tickle
I love my dog.

Vinnie Waghorn (10)
Ifield School, Gravesend

Stomp, Stomp, Stomp

My T-rex can walk
He has got zigzags
Stompy feet
Stomp! Stomp!
Two clawed hands
Wild and furry
Smelly and colourful.

Edward Power (10)
Ifield School, Gravesend

Lenny The Fox

Lenny the fox is orange and bright
He doesn't come alive in daylight
Lenny the fox eats lot of meat
Lots of it is off the street.

Lenny Wood (10)
Ifield School, Gravesend

Power

Power is my name
Liam2 is my nickname
I'm a lazy, crazy dog
I like sausage rolls and crisps.

Liam Hayward (9)
Ifield School, Gravesend

The Do-All Dog

The Do-All Dog does all
It'll dance, it'll tap dance
Through to the moon

Need entertainment?
Call the Do-All Dog
He'll strum to the tune
Through the door
And on the floor

Give it a go in the flow
With the Do-All Dog
Swim with him in the pool
And you might even win the jewel

Time to relax in the cool
Feel all cosy under a blanket
Happy and everything rosy
Until next time for another day
With Do-All Dog.

William Johnson (10)
Monk Fryston CE Primary School, Monk Fryston

The Giant Shnooferb

The giant schnooferb
Cuddles me close in his jet-black fur
I wait and wait every day to hear his rumbling purr
By day he sleeps and sleeps
But by night he creeps around the streets
Searching for the bad guy freaks
In his defence, he uses his electrical tail
Which makes all the baddies wail
The schnooferb has his very own house
That he shares with his toy mouse
The schnooferb house is very large
And the giant schnooferb is always in charge.

Zara Gardner (10)
Monk Fryston CE Primary School, Monk Fryston

Choglephin

Choglephin is the best and no one can change him
He has cheetah legs to win every race he's in
He has a mind like a dolphin to help me with my
homework
He has wings like an eagle to fly me to work
But when I get home, we cuddle up and watch
movies
Because he has comfy dog fur
He has a tail that whacks me
Because it is quite high up
My garden is a mess from Choglephin digging
But he will always be the best pet in the world.

Izzy Newman (10)

Monk Fryston CE Primary School, Monk Fryston

Norbert

N orbert is your worst nightmare, you'll never want to see

O nwards I will talk about how dangerous he can be

R uining land with his giant body and dinosaur wings

B ody of a pig amongst other things

E yes staring back at you whilst shivering with fear

R ipping down trees, he's always near

T ry to avoid him, he may kill. Keep away and then you can chill.

Florence Mitchell (10)
Monk Fryston CE Primary School, Monk Fryston

Oh No! It's Miss Diamond!

I have a cat, she is spoilt
When her money jar is low, she'll have us boiled
She'll put me in a pot and turn up the heat
Then say, "Just gimme the money to spend on the street!"
She has crazy eyes that hypnotise
And she steals all of your money
Her famous line at the end of the day is, "Thanks, honey!"
So I think she's quite a peculiar pet.

Taylor Finlay (10)
Monk Fryston CE Primary School, Monk Fryston

Duck GPA (Guinea Pig Animal)

Duck GPA was a lonely duck
And his guinea pig head looked like the back of a truck

He walked through the wild like a lazy hippo
But his little brain told him to tiptoe

Once he got back to his friend, Trot the Dot
His friend loudly bellowed, "Get in the pot!"

Duck GPA got in the giant pot
And after that, he became a little dot.

Alfie Brewster (10)
Monk Fryston CE Primary School, Monk Fryston

My Peculiar Pet

This beast is extraordinary
But don't be fooled, it is not ordinary
It is not tiny
Or slimy
It will slither
In its wild river
You can try and make it tame
But after, you won't be the same
It is very clever
And will never be injured, never
This creature is not adorable
And is not loveable

But is it your type?

Bryony Taylor (10)
Monk Fryston CE Primary School, Monk Fryston

Johnny

J ohnny is a marvellous creature. He is clever and agile

O n top of Mount Everest is where this monster lives

H e comes in the dead of night and snatches children up

N o one has ever seen him and no one comes back who searches for him

N o man has ever faced him, but are you brave enough?

Y ou may be next!

Will Milne (10)
Monk Fryston CE Primary School, Monk Fryston

Serpon The Giraffe Water Snake

This snake is kind of fake
But it's always awake
It lives in a lake and likes to bake
Its food with its fiery breath
It eats ten meals a day
That's why it's so long
When people are nearby
It sings a song to attract them
And eat them up for its breakfast
Then replace them with feathers.

Max Davies (10)
Monk Fryston CE Primary School, Monk Fryston

This Is Eggo

E xtraordinary, like a butterfly
G igantic, like an elephant
G entle, like a cat
O bsequious, like a dog.

This is Eggo
So great and tall
But as calm as a dog asleep at home
When he is awake
He is as bright as a bird
But when he's asleep
He is never heard.

Olivia Willetts (10)
Monk Fryston CE Primary School, Monk Fryston

Bloodnapper

B reathes fire
L ikes meat
O verexcited to swim
O utrageous tail
D eadly fangs
N ever sleeps
A lways kills
P uts meat in his home
P lays deadly
E ats enormous creatures
R ips trees.

Lewis Brown (11)
Monk Fryston CE Primary School, Monk Fryston

Unidog

U nipup, lazy yet dainty

N ever wakes up before 10am

I nside her glitzy room, you can hear her distinctive snoring

D on't wake her up or you'll be a living sparkle ball

O nly wears pink or purple to bed

G reat as can be, Unidog!

Mia Dawson (10)

Monk Fryston CE Primary School, Monk Fryston

Fishy Boy's Adventure

F ish is as tasty as super salt
I s amazing at fishing
S o he fished a floppy fish
H is favourite fish is funny fish

B ecause it makes him go fish fun mode
O ff the sofa to the sea
Y o, salt makes him go crazy.

Patrick Johnston (10)
Monk Fryston CE Primary School, Monk Fryston

Scpsponga

S uper Ugly is the Scpsponga
C reature-like wings
P urple triangular-shaped eyes
S uperhero like
P erfect hair
O bnoxious attitude
N ight vision
G ood at stealth
A lways kills people.

Leo Judge (10)
Monk Fryston CE Primary School, Monk Fryston

My Peculiar Pet

As mean as a rattlesnake
As sinister as a devil
Not obsequious like a newborn dog
As dangerous as an alien
And as lazy as a sloth
It has ten fangs and 48 teeth
If you ever touch his spiky back
you will slowly die.

Harrison Turner (10)
Monk Fryston CE Primary School, Monk Fryston

The Lazy Cabbit

C at mixed with a rabbit
A lways looking for food
B ecause she is always hungry
B eautiful to look at
I t is a lazy animal
T o a rabbit who can hop to a cat who can jump.

Francesca Cartwright (10)
Monk Fryston CE Primary School, Monk Fryston

Aqua Dog

This dog is dim, but boy can he swim
He is sometimes sad, but don't make him mad
his underwater bark always hits the mark
His favourite food is honey, but only when it's
runny!

Josh Lodge (10)
Monk Fryston CE Primary School, Monk Fryston

Pigeta

A tail so long
A body so strong
A head so small
A leg so tall

A nose so cold
A face so bold
An eye so big
He looks like a pig.

Marissa Braithwaite (10)
Monk Fryston CE Primary School, Monk Fryston

Le Bob Takes Over The World

L ong but fierce
E vil inside

B reakfast he loves
O ne victim couldn't hide
B iscuits is his battle cry...

Hamish Lambeth (10)
Monk Fryston CE Primary School, Monk Fryston

The Blind-Ish Tigertapas

A haiku

Flying through the breeze
Living in the trees and sea
A gentle giant.

Rowan Dawson (10)

Monk Fryston CE Primary School, Monk Fryston

Fire Monster

F ire coming out of his hands
I like to watch him
R ed like a hot potato
E vil horns like points from the bottom of a ruby

M essy monster. When I tidy up he makes another
mess
O nly the greatest mess in the world
N osiest in the town
S limy like a mess of rotten bones
T roublemaker
E xtraordinarily lazy
R otten breath and scales

F erocious claws and as rich as me
L iquidises you in one minute or two
A n incredible, dangerous monster
S lowly he will catch you
H e is annoying.

Nicole King (9)
Newton Primary School, South Ayrshire

Mr Mouse And Inky The Squid

Inky the squid is good at dancing
And you always see him prancing
All around his gorgeous house
And then after that
He goes to meet Mr Mouse
Finally, when he gets home
He gives his luxurious
Light blue hair a careful comb
But before he goes to sleep
He gets some Ben and Jerry's ice cream
And then he goes to bed
For a big, huge dream.

Daniel Jamieson (9)
Newton Primary School, South Ayrshire

Cute Caog

C aog is dangerous like a devil
U nder the dark cave is the caog
T he caog has a very long tail
E ating lots of people

C aog is eating people and going to town
A round the corner the people are dead
O nly the dangerous machine is caog
"G et the caog police now," said the mayor.

Rory Thorrat (8)
Newton Primary School, South Ayrshire

Dinocorn

My dino dances everywhere
If he sees someone he bounces in the air
Then he wants to go to bed
Every night he goes to the vents to get his toy
Oh wait, my dino is a boy
Dino was in the house
There is a mouse
Dino ran to me
He always wakes me up
He eats my food
But the mouse took it and ate it.

Julia Laszczyk (9)
Newton Primary School, South Ayrshire

My Pet's Life

White Elizabeth bounces up and down
And runs everywhere in the town
She feels fluffy and furry
But she's always in a hurry
At night she gets no sleep
In the morning she thinks I am a creep
White Elizabeth likes unicorns
And thinks they eat popcorn.

Alice Balut (9)
Newton Primary School, South Ayrshire

Jaguars

J aguars are cute but feisty.

A nd you can't break a bond with human and jaguar.

G ot to believe they are

U nbelievably magical.

A nd always will be.

R ight because my jaguar is magic.

Bailey Young (9)
Newton Primary School, South Ayrshire

Football Dog

Football dog is black and white.
On the match day he is good or sometimes he is bad.
Tomorrow he is playing at a new team,
balls are good.
He is good at scoring goals,
Logan watches him.

Logan Simpson (9)
Newton Primary School, South Ayrshire

My Peculiar Pet

Spike the spider
Likes to crawl up the wall
And onto the ball
But he's too small
To climb the wall
He needs to call
So he doesn't fall
To get up the wall.

Kai (10)
Newton Primary School, South Ayrshire

Indigo The Superhero Kitty

No way a kitty can be a superhero
Do you know that a cute kitty is a superhero?
Indigo, a clever kitty is a superhero
She is wild, tiny and messy.

Keira Campbell (9)
Newton Primary School, South Ayrshire

Spaceasaurus Rex

S paceasaurus Rex is a dinosaur alien

P lanet Oob is its home

A n invader often gets thrown in a cold pool

C ool creatures live on this planet, such as Gloopysaurus

E ggs are not edible on Planet Oob

A n imposter gets thrown off this planet

S oup is made from acid here

A n object is a baby Oobysaurus

U la is a type of bomb. *Boom!*

R elasauruses are hostile on this planet. *Pow!*

U hiccup is what they say when they hiccup

S eeking warmth is important here. Shiver!

R exysaurus are massive on this planet

E co squads come here to collect plastic on Planet Oob

X phactinuses are prehistoric fish that live on this planet.

Max Smith (9)
Penybont Primary School, Bridgend

Gamersouras Rex

G ood games make him happy

A nd he sometimes eats while playing

M aybe he should stop playing games

E ven if he gets disturbed he won't care

R ows and rows of games he's played

S o much I can't believe his eyes don't hurt

O h my god, he plays until 3am

U nder his pillow, he keeps his games

R unning is what he does sometimes but shortly he goes inside

A lways he gets told to play outside but he just brings his games

S ouras is his middle name

R ings of calls he sometimes ignores

E ven for days and days, he's been playing

X -ray eyes he has but he uses them while laying.

Adam Woolley (8)

Penybont Primary School, Bridgend

The Surprise Under The Sea

Where the north wind meets the sea there's a sea dragon full of memories
The summer sun sizzles over the wind and she is really happy
She loves to drink seaweed and krill smoothies
All her cups are decorated in rubies
Her favourite things to do are eating, sleeping, knitting and writing
Her favourite colours are pink, blue, gold, black and white
Her sharp, slimy and scary teeth are terrible to look at
She thinks that krill is brill
She lives under Pixie Hollow
Her name is Holomor
The snail went for a ride on her tails
She has six short wobbly legs
A unicorn horn and a seahorse head
She wears a white dress with shells on it.

Annabelle Coak (8)
Penybont Primary School, Bridgend

Calrus The Walrus

Calrus the walrus is a marvellous superhero
Calrus is the most sassy superhero ever seen
If you see someone mean
Here he comes
He is sassy but cute
Superhero Calrus
Calrus loves fish
But he has never gotten a kiss
Calrus the walrus has brown and white skin
He doesn't like it
He wishes it could go in the bin
Calrus is really lazy
But when he is fighting crime
He's extraordinary
When he eats sugar he goes crazy
His favourite colour is blue
Because it is the colour of his cape
When there is a robber he is always late.

Ellie Mawer (8)
Penybont Primary School, Bridgend

Space Pug's Life

S pace pugs are robot pugs from Planet Kenozizic

P eople never knew these pugs existed and they are as clever as a troodon

A ll space pugs have weird powers such as trumpet speaker, auto lights, auto siren and toilet plunger grabber

C rawling through the night is still very silly

E very space pug will activate the auto siren and get you, unless tamed

P ick up a metal bone and tame a space pug

yo **U** are pancakes if a space pug kills you

G o and find a space pug to tame.

James Anniss (8)

Penybont Primary School, Bridgend

Whgomstobot

W hgomstobot is a mix of a whale, robot, ghost and hamster

H ates everything, sometimes even himself

G reat at going fast

O mnivorous he calls himself, but only eats meat

M onster he is and likes it too

S mart as Bill Gates

T all as a quarter of the moon

O n the earth, he could cause it to break

B reaking, brawling and banging with everyone and everything

O verall he is the most dangerous thing

T racking everything, no escape.

Carter Morgan (9)

Penybont Primary School, Bridgend

My Big Blue Mouse

B ig-brained mouse
I eat cheese and fish
G ood! It's my favourite dish

B all games are my favourite
L ittle brown mice will be scared of me
U mbrellas won't stop me
E els moving maybe food for me

M arvellous but messy mouse
O n the table's my house
U nder the blue sea, you can't
S ee me
E veryone loves this mouse.

Malachy Jordan (8)
Penybont Primary School, Bridgend

Charlotte The Cheetah

Let me tell you about my pet cheetah
Go deep, deep into the jungle
She lives up a tree but listen to me
She is very hard to find
So listen carefully
I will tell you about her
She has a mouth full of chocolate
And loves it
She has purple eyes
She loves cute hair
Her body is warm and cuddly
She works in Candy Land
In her free time, she goes to the spa
Her tree is like a mansion
It is really big.

Indigo Bevan (8)
Penybont Primary School, Bridgend

Pertul

Pertul is a kind, loving pet
She is fluffy, cute and smart
She lives in the sea
The time I found her
Was when I was swimming
I immediately swam as fast as I could
I started talking
She talked back
I was shocked and she laughed
She said, "Did you not know?"
I said, "No. I never knew."
I asked, "Do you want to come to my house?"
"Okay."

Afsa Chowdhury (8)
Penybont Primary School, Bridgend

Boney And The Tiger

Once there was a dog
He was out on a stroll
His name was Boney
He was very lonely
Until a tiger came upon him
And said, "Give me your owner!"
The tiger raced and chased the dog
The dog went to his owner
While he was on his way
He said, "Go away!"
Bang! Crash! Woof!
Then something happened
They turned into a family.

Sofia Scrowther (8)
Penybont Primary School, Bridgend

Cool Robin

C ola is what my cool robin likes
O n the cool robin, it has a train head
O n the robin, it has a red nose on the train head
L azy robin is super lazy

R obin likes broccoli
O n her is sheepskin
B ouncy balls are her favourite toy
I n her house, there are 50 robins
N aughty robin is super naughty.

Tomasz Bis (8)
Penybont Primary School, Bridgend

My Peculiar Pet

R ocking rainbow rat
A mazing at making rainbows
T iny little rat

My rainbow rat is cute, lazy and sassy
His favourite food is cotton candy
Sometimes he loves to meditate on clouds
He's always calm
He is lovable
He loves new friends
His favourite snack is chewy bones
Sometimes he's wild
My rat loves to race.

Abigail Rumba (7)
Penybont Primary School, Bridgend

Super Turtle

S uper Turtle smells like a skunk
U seful and amazing pet
P et turtle who likes eating
E veryone loves Super Turtle
R olls around in my back garden

T urtles are amazing pets
U nbelievable
R eally cool
T iny and tame
L ovely and stinky
E xtraordinary pet.

Harry Edwards (8)
Penybont Primary School, Bridgend

The Silly Lion

My lion has monkey ears and a unicorn horn
He likes to play hide-and-seek
His favourite food is Oreos
He likes to play with monkey
Lion has a giraffe body
He has 11 eyes
He likes to wear pink dresses
Has 20 legs
Wants to be a hairdresser
He lives in America
He has a zebra head
His favourite treat is pizza and cake.

Sienna Brace (8)
Penybont Primary School, Bridgend

My Adorable Kangaroo

K ind kangaroo likes to be kind

A ngry kangaroo likes being angry

N ervous kangaroo is caring

G reedy kangaroo is called Clawy

A lways kangaroo is sleeping every day

R ude kangaroo is very curious

O range kangaroo is kind and careful

O cean kangaroo likes to eat cake.

Thea Brace (7)

Penybont Primary School, Bridgend

Lulu Leopard

L ulu leopard loves licking lollies
E very day Lulu loves me
O reos are her favourite food
P lease always love your pet
A loving leopard is always around the corner
R un through the forest and you'll find her
D ear me, she can't leave the jungle.

Katy Hill (8)
Penybont Primary School, Bridgend

Combo Panda

C ombo Bonga is catchphrase
O n his head he wears headphones
M rs Panda is his mum
B lack and white
O ne controller

P anda likes bamboo
A nd playing games
N eeds a friend
D o play with him
A nd make him happy.

Joseph Thomas-Bizjak (9)
Penybont Primary School, Bridgend

The Surprise Seal In The Water

Where the north wind reaches the sea
There's a surprise seal in the water
Full of memories
Dive down deep to the sea
The surprise seal in the water is alone
Her favourite food is snow
Her habitat is the Arctic
Her favourite thing to do is play with friends.

Mali James (7)
Penybont Primary School, Bridgend

Dragdopug

D eadly
R uns fast
A ngry ferocious
G rumpy
D angerous digging dog
O bviously, his habitat is in the jungle
P eople are afraid of Dragdopug
U sually lands on his legs
G et yourself a dragdopug.

Tom Beckinsale (8)
Penybont Primary School, Bridgend

Monkey Madness

My monkey lives on the moon
My monkey is mad
My monkey loves maths
My moaning monkey hates melons
My monkey loves McDonald's
My massive monkey is magnificent
My monkey's name is Mos
My monkey loves smashing mugs
My monkey loves mountains.

Arlo Llewellyn (7)
Penybont Primary School, Bridgend

The Secret Sunset

My fox wears socks
Sunset at the beach
Where the llamas leap
Across the northern wind
There lived a fox
He loved to dance
Where the wind beats the sea
My fox's favourite food is waffles
And he is so sure
My fox has lots of friends.

Scarlett Baldwin (7)
Penybont Primary School, Bridgend

My Hot Horse

My horse has hot wings, a horn
And lives in a hot house
She likes hot food
Likes to hum and she is helpful
She loves hot tubs
Loves racing and she's rainbow
Her name is Rocky
She has pink lips and purple eyes
She likes herons and hens.

Marwa Fadel (7)
Penybont Primary School, Bridgend

Peggy And Family

My name is Peggy
I'm always so happy
My dad is called Timmy
My brother is called Limmy
Hello silly, it's Peggy
My sister is called Penny
Penny is so sassy
Sassy is the key
Just be yourself and follow your dreams.

Maisy Searle (8)
Penybont Primary School, Bridgend

Jumping Jake

Jumping Jake is my frog
He lives in a swamp
He didn't eat bugs
I don't know why
But he really loves to jump
Up so high
Up in the sky
He loves to read
He loves to eat
He always spits out the seeds!

Ariandas Poznekovas (8)
Penybont Primary School, Bridgend

The Snake Of The Cake

S taber slips and slops in circles
T ottering, tasering tiny snakes
A mazing actor, amazing snake
B ruised, baked, brave snake
E xercising, evening-loving snake
R apping, raising snake.

Daniel Kocur (8)
Penybont Primary School, Bridgend

Raw

Raw is a rat
He's as tall as a wall
Claws the size of tiger's claws
He likes to have a brawl

He likes causing mischief
He wants to have a war
He likes mythical creatures
He has a massive jaw.

George Evans (9)
Penybont Primary School, Bridgend

The Peculiar Penguin

P enguins love to party
E very pretty penguin
N ever go to ancient Egypt
G rowls at the postman
U nder the purple pond
I n polar places
N esting penguins poo popcorn

Josie John (7)
Penybont Primary School, Bridgend

Jerry Wrestler Tarantula

There was a tarantula
His name was Jerry
His favourite food was berries
It is quite weird
But he had a job
His job is wrestling
And he was good at it
He also liked football
He liked playing it.

Joshua Taylor (8)
Penybont Primary School, Bridgend

Snakey

S cary 10,000-foot tongue
N ever usually bites
A lways tries to slither away
K nows how to fly
E lephants are his favourite food
Y ou must beware, Snakey is everywhere.

Blake Johnson (8)
Penybont Primary School, Bridgend

Luna The Catacorn

This is Luna
Her favourite food is tuna
Her favourite colour is purple
She really likes turtles
She is very energetic
When we give her toys
She gets very hectic
Then they get destroyed.

Chloe Acaster (9)
Penybont Primary School, Bridgend

The Diamond Unicorn

U nique unicorn
N umber one unicorn
I t likes candy
C olourful unicorn
O reos are its favourite candy
R escues people
N ow unicorns are extinct.

Libby McCabe (7)
Penybont Primary School, Bridgend

The Mystery In A Shell

T all and thin
U sed to be a rapper
R unning and very cool
T he place he likes is South Korea
L ittle like a lizard
E xtraordinary and always extra!

Vesta Filipovas (8)
Penybont Primary School, Bridgend

Marvellous And Strange Racoon

R avishing and clever
A dorable and feisty
C reative and cruel
O ctober is his favourite month
O ffensive and mean sometimes
N aughty and strong.

Ava Folley (8)
Penybont Primary School, Bridgend

Sarah The Vet

S arah works at the vet
A mazing and British accent
R acing cars. She likes dog food
A nd has 15 long legs
H as three pink eyes and has purple skin.

Ethan Ellis (8)
Penybont Primary School, Bridgend

The Underworld

S ometimes he smokes colours
A lways eats Oreos
B ouncing, boozing, playing with baboons
R ich, rude, he likes food
E xtraordinary eating whales.

George Wyatt (7)
Penybont Primary School, Bridgend

The Sleepy Spotty Snake

I love my silly snake
I love my spotty snake
I love my small snake
I love my sneaky snake
I love my smart snake
I love my scary snake
My sticky snake loves me.

Emily Dinham (8)

Penybont Primary School, Bridgend

The Dangerous Jeff

D iamond necklace

R ed eyes like lava

A mazing

G oes to Cardiff matches

O reos are his favourite food

N o is his favourite word.

Sam Alford (8)
Penybont Primary School, Bridgend

My Growing Guinea Pig

I love my guinea pig
My guinea pig is gorging green grapes
I love my gorgeous guinea pig
I love my grey guinea pig
I love my guinea pig
My guinea pig is lovely.

Olivia Davidson (7)
Penybont Primary School, Bridgend

Lovely Rabbit

R ed rabbit runs

A nd rides a rocket

B eautiful bunny

B asket of eggs

I like rabbits

T omorrow the rabbit rides a rock.

Theo Morris (7)
Penybont Primary School, Bridgend

Bonkers Beagle

I love my bored beagle
I love my beautiful beagle
I love my black beagle
I love my brilliant beagle
I love my blind beagle
I love my bleeding beagle.

Anthony Cammish (7)
Penybont Primary School, Bridgend

Weird Kangaroo

My crafty kangaroo
My clumsy kangaroo
My colourful kangaroo
My kind kangaroo
My cute kangaroo
My caring kangaroo
I really love kangaroos.

Ollie Newman (7)
Penybont Primary School, Bridgend

The Mighty Monkey

My muddy monkey love me
My monkey is a mad monkey
My monster monkey made a mood monkey
My monkey met a meal monkey
My monkey made McDonald's.

Amber Jarvie (7)
Penybont Primary School, Bridgend

Kind Koala

K ung-fu koala

O n the wall, there was a koala

A pples they eat

L ove my cute koala

A mazing karate koala.

Hannah Hughes (8)
Penybont Primary School, Bridgend

Chatter Cheetah

My cheetah has a head of a dinosaur
He goes high and he has sharp teeth
He's got long legs
Runs fast
He chatters all day long.

Kaelan Hurley (9)
Penybont Primary School, Bridgend

African Armadillo

I love my agile armadillo
My armadillo likes angry ants
He picks apples around my ankles
Armadillos are always athletic.

Harri Bartlett (7)
Penybont Primary School, Bridgend

Larry The Lion

L arry is ferocious
I n the jungle he lives
O h no! He is climbing a tree
N aughty Larry!

George Gale (8)

Penybont Primary School, Bridgend

My Peculiar Pet

I love my cheeky cheetah
My cheetah chases chickens
To Cardiff, my cheetah chucks
Computers out of the church.

Chase Hurley (7)
Penybont Primary School, Bridgend

Lovely Lion

I love my laughing lion
I love my friendly lion
I love my lovely lion
My lion loves me
I love my lion.

Charlie Harrison (7)
Penybont Primary School, Bridgend

Jaws Is A Vampire Bunny

J aws is a vampire
A ferocious lazy bunny
W eird and wild
S neaky Jaws the bunny.

Jesse Jones (8)
Penybont Primary School, Bridgend

The Fat Frog

F rench frog
R unning with a fireball
O range fiery flames
G oes fish frying.

Charlie Sims (7)
Penybont Primary School, Bridgend

Toby The Dog Fish

T oby the dog fish

O nly pet I love

B lue colour dog fish

Y ou are the best!

Jorja Payne (8)
Penybont Primary School, Bridgend

The Peculiar Dragon

S ausages are its favourite food
A fter he eats sausages, he always parties
F erocious at times but not always
A ddiction to hot dogs
R ips out the sausage first
E yesight of a hawk

L oves to party when there's a space on the dance floor
O h, he loves people at times, not always
V ets always scare him because of needles
E very day for breakfast he eats hot dogs
S ecure for a bodyguard

M entions to get hot dogs whenever we go out
E ats all the food every day.

Jasmine Breakwell (9)
St Bartholomew's CE Primary School, Stourport-On-Severn

My Manic Dragon

My manic dragon is amazing
When he plays he's really crazy
When he eats he is very messy
But when he talks he's really sassy
When it's rainy he is really lazy
But when you see him he's really scaly
His favourite food is fish and chips
But he can't let them touch his lips
Splash! He's in the water
He only fills the bath to a quarter
Creak! The manic dragon opens the door
He walks lots more and more
After the walk, he heads back home
To have a nap all alone!

Emily Rix (9)
St Bartholomew's CE Primary School, Stourport-On-Severn

The Ice Crystal Dragon

The ice crystal, shimmering dragon was called
Crystal
One day we went to a cave
The cave was as dark as a shimmering freezing
piece of ice
We went for a mythical fly to find another baby
dragon
His name was Ice Dragon
He was sleeping on the mommy dragon
The mommy dragon felt sleepy so they gathered
together
Then suddenly they heard a big stomp
It was the daddy dragon who had a friendly
dragon for the baby dragon
Last but not least, Daddy dragon snuggled
together and went to sleep.

Shannon Shurmer (8)
St Bartholomew's CE Primary School, Stourport-On-Severn

The Holiday Dragon That Gets Pranked!

A long time ago there was a holiday dragon
She went to the beach
However, she doesn't like water
Splash!
Someone pushed her
"I'm going to get you, you beast!"
Lying on the sand, waiting like a hungry tiger
She caught a glimpse of something from the
corner of her eye
It was a peculiar beast as tall as a skyscraper
Quietly sneaking up on him and she scares him
with her tiger roar
With that, he fell straight into the sea and floated
away.

Olivia Houghland (8)
St Bartholomew's CE Primary School, Stourport-On-Severn

My Peculiar Pet

I have a peculiar pet
He keeps popping out on me
Going to clown concerts and learning to say, "I rule!"
This peculiar pet happens to be a red, spiky dragon
Who dresses up in a clown costume
Dancing to disco DJs around the world
Eating spicy hot dogs as fast as lightning
Burp! A red puff of breath fills the air
He travels night and day
To find his dream mansion.

Kayla Cable (9)
St Bartholomew's CE Primary School, Stourport-On-Severn

My Peculiar Pet

A long time ago there was a monstrous dragon
With scales as sharp as an iceberg
Teeth as sharp as a megalodon's teeth
And monstrous, crispy breath
Wings as long as a giraffe's neck
She camouflages into the grass
When monstrous, terrifying knights
Come looking for her
In the summer she hides
So she can recharge her ability to fly.

Peter-Roy Winters (8)
St Bartholomew's CE Primary School, Stourport-On-Severn

Ice Dragon

I was going to bed when I saw something blue
The tiny dragon's enemy is Racoon
It would go in cold areas
That's where he can freeze
She is cute but weird
Because she sleeps in the day
Cold food is what it eats
Hot food is its weakness
his name is Ethan
And he is an ice professional
Hockey he plays every day of the week.

Zach Williams (8)
St Bartholomew's CE Primary School, Stourport-On-Severn

Zooming Dragonfly

Ice Dragon was flying and spying
The cold, icy dragon was in the white snow
The ice dragon drifted towards the ice water
Claws scratched lines in the snow
Footprints lay beneath the snow
Telling people where he'd been
Slowly he walked into the freezing water
Quick as a flash, he turns into a zooming
dragonfly.

Jorge Cook (8)

St Bartholomew's CE Primary School, Stourport-On-Severn

Shelley The Messy Dragon

S helley is so messy if you wanted to know Shelley Dragon

s **H** e is wild

E lla is her friend

L illie is Ellie's best friend

L illie likes ice cream, Shelley loves ice cream

E mily is so funny, Shelley and Emily are BFFs

Y ummy rice is Shelley's favourite food.

Cassie Mai Tovey (8)
St Bartholomew's CE Primary School, Stourport-On-Severn

Ninja Dragons

My ninja dragons are eerie black
Their names are Will and Nala
They like to sneak out at night
They like to help the cops and stop crime
I know it's weird having dragons as ninjas
But when they go to the park and play catch
Remember when duty calls
They're known as Shadow and Sunset.

William Stanley (8)
St Bartholomew's CE Primary School, Stourport-On-Severn

Speedy Dragon

This dragon can't be seen, he is that fast
But people can hear him
He goes all around the world
He eats while he is running
His weakness is slow things or him going slow
His arch-nemesis is Slowie Mowie
His name is Speedy
When he sees his arch-nemesis
The arch-nemesis will be gone.

Oliver Bird (8)
St Bartholomew's CE Primary School, Stourport-On-Severn

The Song Wing

The cute, colourful dragon has a voice like a siren
To lure her prey she hypnotises them
Once they are there she makes them sing to her
Along with her beautiful singing voice
Everybody sings and dances with her
The beautiful wings start to change colours
Which looks like a musical rainbow.

Polly Walton (8)
St Bartholomew's CE Primary School, Stourport-On-Severn

The Ice Queen

She skates across the carpet of ice
She decorates the frozen pond
She likes to go and get ice fish
She has had 33,004,500 people to eat
Her breath is freezing cold like frozen ice
She could turn people into freezing cold deadly ice
She is so, so cold like the top of mountains.

Charlie Lippitt (8)
St Bartholomew's CE Primary School, Stourport-On-Severn

The Gaming Dragon

D ragon called Diamond loved gaming
I t inspired her to become a YouTuber
A ll day she sat at the computer
M onday came, all her fans gathered
O n her birthday, Diamond made a video
N o one came to her party
D iamond felt unhappy.

Lillie-Mae Mae Adams (8)
St Bartholomew's CE Primary School, Stourport-On-Severn

The Crystal Dragon

The Crystal Dragon was shimmering
She was like a diamond in the sky
Rosie was a kind dragon
Helping everyone in trouble
Sometimes Rosie found it hard
To help everyone all the time
Rosie then went to see her friends
Before she went to Dragon School.

Molly Foster (8)
St Bartholomew's CE Primary School, Stourport-On-Severn

Enternator

Enternator is a peculiar pet
He hides in the darkness
If you see him he will use a powerful move
If is called Diamax Cannon
It shoots glitter everywhere
This time it will spray you gold
The pet is very mysterious and weird
He is the Enternator.

Jacob Price (8)
St Bartholomew's CE Primary School, Stourport-On-Severn

The Crystal Dragon

S he was made out of crystals

H er job is a famous gamer

W hen she hunts, she looks her prey in the eye

T hen pounces and jumps and bites into it

A fter licking her lips from the blood

S he returns to her crystal cave.

Suleekha Ibrahim (8)
St Bartholomew's CE Primary School, Stourport-On-Severn

Ripper Roo

Ripper Roo is a very crazy kangaroo
With blue fur and floppy ears
Has sharp teeth and a drippy tongue
Obsessed with explosives
Even though he lacks the ability to use his arms
Because he has a straight jacket on
his arch-nemesis is Crash Bandicoot.

Conor Leach (9)
St Bartholomew's CE Primary School, Stourport-On-Severn

The Rock Dragon

He likes to party and he likes to dance
He dances wherever he goes
The Rock Dragon flies through the trees
He rocks everywhere
He's colourful and bright
His teeth are as sharp as a carrot
He plays the guitar and he's a rockstar!

Tobias Griffiths (8)
St Bartholomew's CE Primary School, Stourport-On-Severn

Glamorous Dragon

Stomp! Stomp! A big, big dragon
On top of the trees, he stood
It is a glamorous dragon
Who dresses in fancy suits
He likes people who dance a lot
And drops food when he feeds people.

Jake Curzey (8)
St Bartholomew's CE Primary School, Stourport-On-Severn

The World Of The Ice Dragon

She skates across the carpet
Then decorates the frozen pond
She likes the winter to recharge her icy veins
She licks her lips like a hungry dragon
She stares at the prey while watching intensely.

Carlton Harper (8)
St Bartholomew's CE Primary School, Stourport-On-Severn

The Organ Dragon

He plays football for a professional team
Midfield is where he is best
No game has he lost
That's why they are in the Premier League
To get energy he eats rice
But hates eating ice.

Alfie Short (8)
St Bartholomew's CE Primary School, Stourport-On-Severn

Peculiar Dragon

My peculiar dragon he was silly
He sleeps upside down
He is so silly he can't even fly
Because he can't stop laughing
He always flies sideways
He hurts his head and laughs.

Ellie May Mason (8)
St Bartholomew's CE Primary School, Stourport-On-Severn

The Ice Crystal Dragon

One snowy sunset night
My mum kissed me goodnight
When she left I gave her a hug
Leaving a crystal dragon behind
It has icicles razor-sharp
And it has frost for breath.

Darcie Lees (8)
St Bartholomew's CE Primary School, Stourport-On-Severn

The Bike-Riding Dragon

The dragon was riding his bike
Mommy Dragon shouted, "Food is ready!"
Timothy jumped off his bike to get his food
He went to the shop for some clothes.

Charlie Coglan (8)
St Bartholomew's CE Primary School, Stourport-On-Severn

Doris The Dancing Dragon

Doris the dragon
Was looking outside the window
She saw a wizard
Dressed like a unicorn.

Kia Sutcliffe (8)
St Bartholomew's CE Primary School, Stourport-On-Severn

Baldy Funny Minecraft Dragon

Baldy Funny dragon
Breathed ice fire
He flew around the forest
Freezing all the trees.

Alfie Walker

St Bartholomew's CE Primary School, Stourport-On-Severn

The Incredibly Dangerous Tarantula

Once there was a tarantula
He had lovely green and black stripes
But he doesn't know any rhymes
His name is Duncan and he can poison
People don't want him to save the day
Because they've got Super Simon
He can rob, jump and sing
But I use him as a spring
He can dance and prance
He can do all sorts
I love him because he is him
Even though he might be behind you
Love him, please
He can do all sorts and he's my bestie
So treat him with love, please
He isn't really dangerous
He's my friend
You can find him in Candy Land.

Noah Callow (8)

St Edward's Catholic Academy, Swadlincote

The Lazy Dog Called Laze Clever

Once there was a dog called Laze Clever
She was lazy but she was clever
She was crazy
She bumps and hops everywhere around
She loves stuff that is round
She sucks a pound
She does an oopsy daisy
Dancing to the sky with a pie
She sings like a star in space
Laze sang a nice cute song
She was as crazy as a silly goat
Then she said a big, giant, massive goodbye
Then she crashed in a tree
The fire engine needed to
Come to get her off the tree.

Victoria Malinowska (8)
St Edward's Catholic Academy, Swadlincote

Great Perry, The Platypus

I brought a platypus
That was as tiny as a dog
But just like a frog
Its name is Perry
He likes to go on the ferry
He's extraordinarily clever
He's just as cute as a newt
It's scaly and waily
And it's just as lazy as you
But he does normally have a big poo
Maybe a bit like you
He had a friend that likes a slight bend
He likes some food
And always takes a quick snooze.

Sebastian Brown (8)
St Edward's Catholic Academy, Swadlincote

The Balancing Dog

Once I adopted a dog
His name is Vince and he can wink
He can ride a bike with cake on his back
He's a little furious dog and he's clever
He can run as fast as a speedboat
He howls at night
So I get him cake to balance on his back
We run around the garden with each other
We play all night and he sleeps in the day.

Ivy-Bo Fogg (8)
St Edward's Catholic Academy, Swadlincote

The Jelly Sausage Spiky Monster

He lurks in the darkness ready to pounce on prey
He has slimy jelly legs that make your skin squirm
He smells like rotting, festering fish
He moves, slithering and squelching
Leaving behind a trail of stinking, squelchy slime
He roars like a tiger's tummy
His personality is grumpy, lazy, messy and ferocious
His favourite food is cheeky children
You think he is a nice, friendly giant
But actually, inside he's a wild, clawed, dangerous monster
His body is sticky, spiky and shiny
He gobbles you up in one bite
and you go slithering down his spine
Covered in cheeky children gloop
His spine is so agile you can't hold on
He lives in a volcano
His neck is one kilometre long
So his head is above the clouds.

Raphaelle Leigh-Davies (9)

St Edward's Royal Free Ecumenical Middle School, Windsor

Noodles The Noodle

There once was a cocker spaniel called Noodles
But people called her Noods
But this black and white dog didn't like any sort of doggy food
Noodles loved noodles and the house was full of noodles galore
And she would shout (in doggy language) "I want more, more, more!"
She would gobble them down with her floppy ears and waggy tail
If she eats a few more she'll become the size of a whale
Later on that day, Noodles sat on the sofa with Clara, her owner
Not to be rude but she was a bit of a moaner
Especially after being set homework by Miss Parker
In which she was finishing with a marker
Then Clara saw something crazy
Because normally Noodles was lazy
But she was running around and being crazy and stretchy
Which was super extraordinary

Day by day, Noodles turned more noodle-y
And Clara's mum called the vets worriedly
They said there was nothing they could do
So they sent her home with a toy and a chew
But Clara said, "I don't care because I love my Noods
She's a very cool little dude!"

Clara Zuk (9)
St Edward's Royal Free Ecumenical Middle School, Windsor

The Dog With No Bark

I have a dog called Storm
One night we went for a walk
But it was summer, so it was warm
I told Storm to be good but she ate some chalk
This is a disaster
Was my only thought
But soon I couldn't stop myself
And I abounded into laughter
When we got to dog A&E
They checked she was okay
Then we were off, yippee
But they said she had to stay
The night she came back was a very happy night
But I had to buy some medicine
She didn't like it but I guess that serves her right
Then one day she wasn't barking
She wasn't usually like this
Then I realised she couldn't bark at all
But it didn't seem to stop her larking around.

Averil Newton (10)
St Edward's Royal Free Ecumenical Middle School, Windsor

The Happy Huffer

My pet is peculiar
He's strange but kind
I love him because
He is one of a kind
Everyone says he's a very odd creature
But I'll tell you
some of his interesting features
He has a very short neck
And a very green tongue
He's quite old now
But he used to be young
With extremely long legs and lilacy fur
Toes curly and covered in pinky hair
His skin is quite lumpy, a bit like a toad
And traffic upsets him when we walk near the road
So my pet's one-off, so special, unique
But I love him and need him even though he's a
freak.

Liliana Baxendale (9)
St Edward's Royal Free Ecumenical Middle School, Windsor

The Monster Pet

A creature lurks in the darkness of a shadow
It has bulging red eyes with big black flies
It has a long sloppy drool like a hideous ghoul
Its grimy claws are nothing compared to its slimy jaws
It's super smelly with a really fat belly
It possesses long, brown feathery wings and other disgusting little things
It has filthy black fur and when you stroke it, it will begin to purr
It has a high-pitched screech and always sucks on people's legs like a leech
It leaps inside bins and survives on leftover fish skins
It goes by the name of Bish, like a dish of fish.

Elena Littlewood (10)
St Edward's Royal Free Ecumenical Middle School, Windsor

This Is My Pet

My peculiar pet is pink
And is good at playing hide-and-seek
Sometimes she makes a mess
But when it comes to swimming
She is the best

My peculiar pet is marvellous and smart
And can even balance on a big ball

My pet is peculiar to me
Because she's scared of bees
And doesn't like the sea
When I ask her what should I wear
She looks at me hesitantly
My pet is amazing and adorable to me
In case you haven't guessed
My pet is a pig, my pig, Penelope.

Grace Fowler (10)
St Edward's Royal Free Ecumenical Middle School, Windsor

Tiny Tinker The Terrific Tortoise

Tinker is my tortoise
Some tortoises are enormous
But Tinker is tiny
He is only a baby
But he is not normal
He is magical
In the night
He is a wonderful sight
Because...
He is a shape-shifter
He can be anything he wants to be
A clever crocodile
A gigantic guinea pig
A slimy serpent
An agile ant
A colourful koala
So every night is a new adventure
And there you have it
Tiny Tinker, my terrific tortoise.

Robyn Calver (10)
St Edward's Royal Free Ecumenical Middle School, Windsor

Cattypillar

This is Cattypillar, my peculiar pet
You should see the strange looks we get at the vets
Although she walks like a caterpillar
She has the rhythm of a sassy cat
You would expect her to eat green leaves
She much prefers a furry rat
She has an adorable face
But sadly, a slimy back
How very lucky I am
To own such an incredible pet
So colourful and clever
But the weirdest animal I've ever met!

Olivia Rutland (10)
St Edward's Royal Free Ecumenical Middle School, Windsor

My Peculiar Cat

I have a cat
She is a peculiar cat
She dances on shelves
And swings on trees
She has glitter skin
And rainbow knees
Her fur smells like
Bubblegum sweets
She is sassy but classy
And she walks like a queen
She is the most peculiar cat
You have ever seen!

Sienna Simpson (9)
The Glapton Academy, Nottingham

My Pet

I have a pet, she is a mouse
She scuttles all over the house
We call her Lucy as you see
She is as messy as can be
Tightrope walking is her skill
For her to win a competition is my will
Cheese is her favourite food
She is never in a bad mood
I once mistook her for a rat
And she was nearly eaten by a cat
I once painted her red
And poured orange paint over her head
Together we have so much fun
We jump, we skip, we hop, we run
She's the best pet I've ever had
She brings me so much love.

Yisroel Dov Bor Weitz (9)
Tiferes Shlomo Boys' School, Hendon

Rufus

R ufus always likes to be
U nder control from his
F riendly owner
U ri Hacrooton is his
S ibling

H e is a very nice pet
A nd he is also very
C alm and special
R ufus is not very red, but his
O wner's best colour is red
O bviously, he weighs a lot of tons and pounds
T oday he weighs a bit less because he went
O n a diet
N ow we know about Uri and Rufus!

Mendy Friedman (9)
Tiferes Shlomo Boys' School, Hendon

Rufus Hacrooton

R ufus always likes to be
U nder control from his
F riendly and kind owner
U ri Hacrooton is his beloved
S ibling

H e is a very nice pet
A nd is also very
C alm and special
R ufus is not very red, but his
O wner's best colour is red
O bviously, he weighs a lot of
T ons and pounds and he keeps it all
O n his desk
N ow we know about Rufus and Uri!

Chaim Roth (9)
Tiferes Shlomo Boys' School, Hendon

Here Comes The King

B ugatti dog
U ses his day driving in the streets. He
G oes here, he goes there
A nd he doesn't help me, so
T oday I
T old him to help me and
I would give him extra petrol

D og helped me with some errands, but the
O ther errands I had to do myself, so I
G ot up from my sleep and did it myself.

Shmuli Grosshass (9)
Tiferes Shlomo Boys' School, Hendon

Squirrel

He's gentle
But not mental
He's cute
Because he's mute
He eats nuts
But has no cuts
He's scared
But carefully cared
He runs
But likes buns
He's scared of a bear
And won't sit on a chair
He can run a mile
Even through a pile.

Chesky Feiner (9)
Tiferes Shlomo Boys' School, Hendon

Lions

Beware of Brodus Stridus the lion
When he's hungry he can kill
So give him his fill
His body is burly
And his hair is curly
He is clever
Stupid he is never
He eats meat
But beef is his favourite treat
He sleeps all day
To keep him okay.

Menachem Weisz (9)
Tiferes Shlomo Boys' School, Hendon

Budgies

Max's legs are red like a tomato
Though he looks like a potato
He might be a budgie
Though he feels very muggy
He might be feathery
But he is not scary
He might be green
But he is not mean.

Sruli Tesler (9)
Tiferes Shlomo Boys' School, Hendon

Georgina, My Flamingo

F un pet
L oves to play
A nd likes to eat
M ashed potatoes
I nteresting pet
N othing misses her eye
G o flamingo
O ff you go!

Shmuli Roth (10)

Tiferes Shlomo Boys' School, Hendon

Longy

Longy is my name
Of course, I'm very tame
I only eat bats
Although I'm not so fat
Beware, I am still dangerous.

Chaim Heller (9)
Tiferes Shlomo Boys' School, Hendon

The Farrago Fox

The farrago fox was a peculiar pet
It would lick your hand if you were upset
It was winsome and colourful all around its body
But sometimes it would lie in the mud: very shoddy
Its marvellous fur was littered at times
Then it would scratch and sigh out whines
You would have to scrub its fur with bottles of
soap
Then the fox would just have to keep hope
It would then leap out of the bath, run into the hall
Go into the living room, and stand up tall
It would feel proud and soft as once before
For he was again the animal everyone would adore
Maybe in the future, farrago fox
To avoid getting dirty, wear your socks

Alexander Vanbrabant (9)
Westminster Cathedral Choir School, Westminster

Super Saffi!

There once was a dog called Saffi
Who was very, very happy.
She had superpowers
And she really liked flowers
She flew with flowers
And danced with flowers
And did everything with flowers
Always using her superpowers
She was the best friend you could ever have
She could go anywhere
Without a wrong turn, like sat nav
Saffi always saved the day
And always had time to play
Saffi could fly anywhere in the world
She was absolutely absurd
Everywhere she went, the sun was always out
And she sniffed things out with her marvellous
snout.

Jasper Channell (9)
Westminster Cathedral Choir School, Westminster

The Unique Tiger

Oh, I've never seen a tiger so lazy
Sleeping much more than a baby
Oh, I've never seen a tiger so grumpy
With his stripes so furry and bumpy
Oh, I've never seen a tiger so ferocious
Getting so fierce when others say he's atrocious
Just a warning: don't wake him up
Otherwise he'll spill your cup
When he's angry, he roars so loud
He sees his prey and he chases you around
You can hear him ten miles away and there's no doubt.

James Simpson (9)
Westminster Cathedral Choir School, Westminster

My Disobedient Cockroach

My cockroach always stays inside
Trying to hide from me taking him outside
He always hides under the sofas
Trying to get away
But in the end, he finally does
And the next day, here we go again
My cockroach is very naughty
He never wants to go outside
Even when his hair is knotty
He never ever goes outside
Never will, never wants to
All he does is sit inside
Doing whatever he minds
Like sleeping and being
My disobedient cockroach.

Vincent Vogel (10)
Westminster Cathedral Choir School, Westminster

Douglas The Doctor

Douglas was incredibly smart
He could do any equations
And he had a big heart
He answered people's questions
And helped anyone who needed it
Douglas was an extraordinary doctor
He was a superhero with a scalpel
And his patients were always nurtured
But he could only treat fellow turtles
He could heal any injury or illness
His medicines were like potions
And he could perform surgery easily
But his turtle legs slowed him down.

Kei Endo (9)
Westminster Cathedral Choir School, Westminster

Rocky The Dog

My dog, Rocky, is a brave, strong dog
He loves saving people from the monsters of the
bog
His big weighty tummy gets bigger every day
Because he eats all the bills that I need to pay
And he eats dog food ten times per day
He has tonnes of friends who are all bullies
But after years, they all went friendly
Rocky loves Frisbees which are all red
But they always fly to the dusty shed
My brave, strong dog is my best

Guanting Luo (9)
Westminster Cathedral Choir School, Westminster

Savage Shark

My shark is a savage shark
It hits the glass and makes a mark
I think I should let it go into the wild
But I don't think its manners would be very mild
It looks at me with resentful eyes and ragged jaws
I would think that it's against the law to hold a
shark
So I will let it go
Oh no! It bit my toe
Help me, help me!
He's getting to my knee.

Laurence Stiles (10)
Westminster Cathedral Choir School, Westminster

Sammy The Sloth

Sammy the sloth yawns all day
He is so tired that he cannot play
He is so small he can fit in your hand
But he is always so happy, his smile so grand
He hangs from great heights
Even for many nights
He has two tiny toes
And a very big nose
Sammy lives in the wild
And likes to sleep when it's mild
Because he is only a child.

Henry Talalla (9)
Westminster Cathedral Choir School, Westminster

Mr Wiggly Whale The Tattletale

Once there was a whale
Called Wiggly Whale
He was such a tattletale
Once Wiggly was so pale
Because he had a white tail
Tattletales are little whales
That eat only fishes' scales
Whales are such tattletales
Because they drink from the Holy Grail
Whales are scared of other whales
Because they're dressed in chainmail.

Max Billet (9)
Westminster Cathedral Choir School, Westminster

Mighty Wither

Here he stomps his foot
And the hard ground shakes
He yawns and the glass breaks
And the birds fly away
From his golden fur and his silver claws.
He can transform into anything
His legendary eyesight is better than an eagle's
He lays his eggs then he watches until they hatch
And stays with them until they find a match.

John Stoner (9)
Westminster Cathedral Choir School, Westminster

Partying Peter

He parties and never stops
Only to take a nap or two
He loves the pops and fizzy whizzes
That the multicoloured balloons make
You won't find him in the zoo
You'll only find him baking at cakes
He'll play until night comes
And then he'll flop down
In his bed and dream
Of partying all the night.

Tomas Trenor (9)
Westminster Cathedral Choir School, Westminster

My Super-Fast Snail

I've got a super-fast snail
He's got an engine which can't fail
He goes faster than a hawk
And he eats a tonne of pork
In a week
He never feels weak
He can outrun a cheetah
After having a fajita
And he can gobble up a whale
After lugging a pail
For a hundred miles
Over terracotta tiles.

Adam Harris (9)
Westminster Cathedral Choir School, Westminster

Rainbow Dog

Rainbow Dog is as colourful as Skittles
He reminds you of when you were little
Rainbow Dog brightens your day
And is with you all the way
Rainbow Dog is fluffy
And makes you happy
When you have worries
Rainbow Dog listens to your stories
Rainbow Dog is a true friend
And it will never end.

Loïc Lenoble (9)
Westminster Cathedral Choir School, Westminster

Spectacular Spoof

S pectacular Spoof lives in a den, a

P layful pen where he has a friend called Ben. He's an

O bedient animal who never gives up. An

O dd boy who has a toy. A

F unny chap, he smiles for joy!

Alejandro Maqueda Martin (9)
Westminster Cathedral Choir School, Westminster

YOUNG wRITERS
INFORMATION

We hope you have enjoyed reading this book – and that you will continue to in the coming years.

If you're a young writer who enjoys reading and creative writing, or the parent of an enthusiastic poet or story writer, do visit our website **www.youngwriters.co.uk**. Here you will find free competitions, workshops and games, as well as recommended reads, a poetry glossary and our blog. There's lots to keep budding writers motivated to write!

If you would like to order further copies of this book, or any of our other titles, then please give us a call or order via your online account.

Young Writers
Remus House
Coltsfoot Drive
Peterborough
PE2 9BF
(01733) 890066
info@youngwriters.co.uk

Join in the conversation!
Tips, news, giveaways and much more!

 **YoungWritersUK**    **@YoungWritersCW**